From the Author of: The Insider's Guide: Getting a Fresh Financial Start in Utah

LIFE AFTER BANKRUPTCY

THE GAME PLAN TO REBUILD, RESTORE AND RENEW YOUR CREDIT AFTER BANKRUPTCY

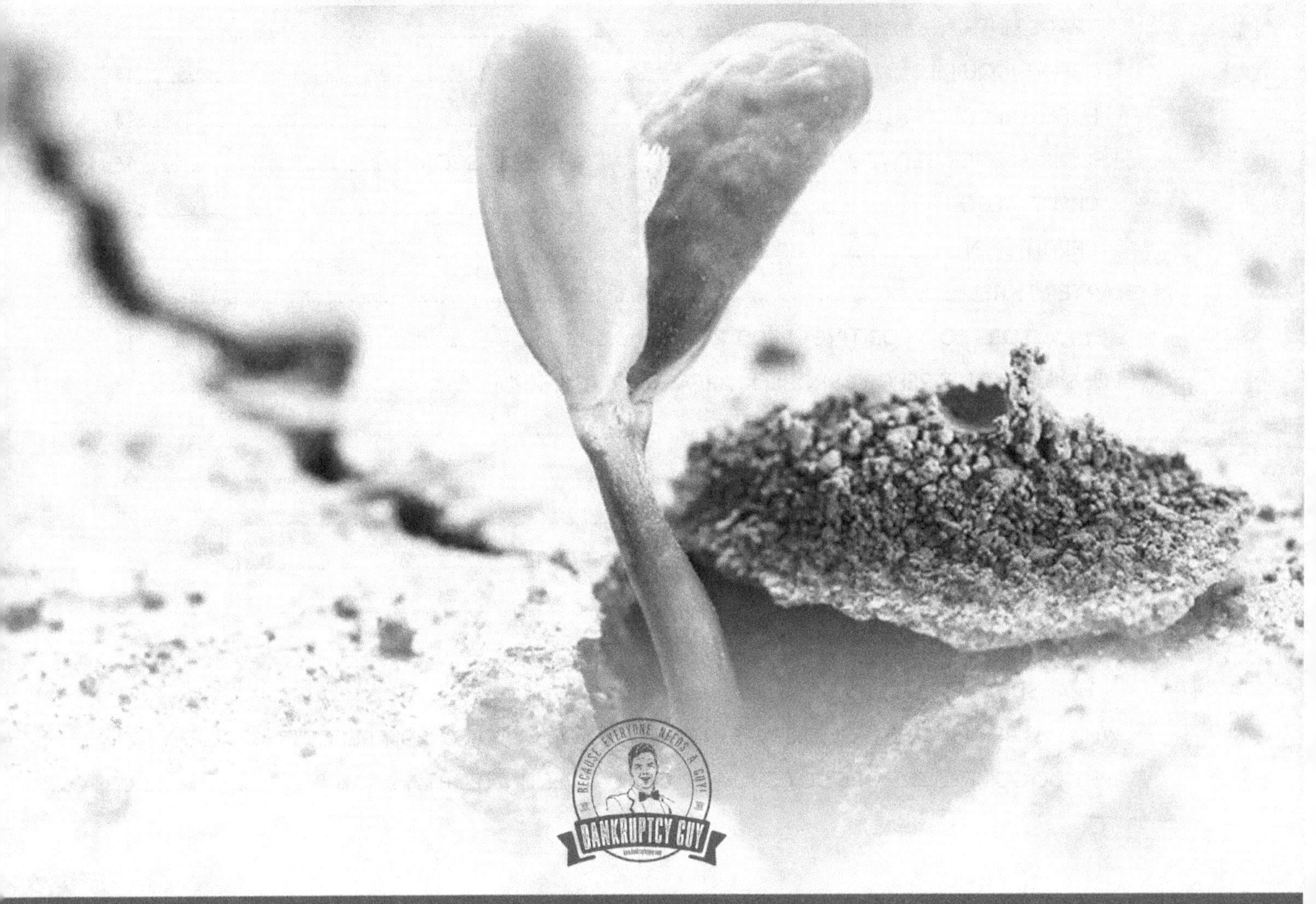

By Douglas Barrett, Esq

CONTENTS

FORWARD

I have worked with thousands of people who are drowning, day in and day out, under the weight of their financial problems. Since 2000 I have helped most of them breathe again by filing for bankruptcy protection under the U.S. Bankruptcy Code and obtain a fresh financial start. Yet, at the same time, I have watched a number of my former clients continue to struggle to rebuild their lives after bankruptcy. As I started to look into the problem further, I found that for most of them, this ongoing struggle was for the simple reason they didn't come up with a game plan after their bankruptcy to get back on track with their finances.

In this country for some reason it is assumed that everyone is born with an inner financial advisor like a Warren Buffett that tells us intuitively how to manage our money. Let me be the first to tell you this is not the case. Personal financial skills are learned not breed within us, because of this, I have set out in this book to help you learn some key post-bankruptcy financial skills so you will not just survive after filing bankruptcy but actually thrive after bankruptcy.

The layout of this book includes information on credit and credit reporting, the next section is dedicated to helping you navigate the major credit bureaus and how to challenge incorrect information on your credit history and finally the last section is dedicated to helping you develop a game plan to get your financial life back. There is no secret or magical way to get a perfect credit score by going to some secret website and paying hundreds of dollars to come up with an easy fix. If that were available I would point you in that direction. By the way anyone that tells you they can do it that way is scamming you. Thankfully the fix is actually simple, straight forward, and included in your personal Game Plan at the end of the book. So let me assure you if you will follow a few simple steps there is actually life after bankruptcy!

All the best,

Douglas "The Bankruptcy Guy" Barrett,

Attorney at Law

Special thanks to the input received from Attorney Philip Jones,

the aid of my Research Assistant Bethany Allen

and of course my dog Zeus.

CHAPTER ONE

DO I REALLY NEED CREDIT?

You have just filed a bankruptcy due to financial problems with credit, creditors and/or credit cards or overwhelming medical debt and have said to yourself that you will never *no way no how* use credit again. Most likely you are gun shy of banks, credit unions and high pressure lenders and want to move forward on a cash only basis. You may have even said to yourself that you will never get into the credit game again. I understand and believe me I know where you are coming from.

If you are like the vast majority of people wanting to thrive financially after a bankruptcy you will need to establish some kind of credit history. For example if you ever want to take out a loan for school, buy a home, open a credit card so you can rent a car or just about anything that requires borrowing money then a good credit history is essential.

For example if your goal is to buy a home, unless you have cash to pay for it in full when you buy it, you are going to need someone to spot you the money so you can purchase the home. You might have rich parents or a relative willing to loan you the money but this tends to be a rare occurrence. Most of us need to go to a lender (ie, bank, mortgage company or credit union) to get the financial back-up needed to buy a home.

Different kinds of lenders have different rules in place as to how and who they will help buy a home. The one thing they have in common is this: they want to know that you will be able to repay them - thus the need to have a "credit history". A longer and more positive credit history will make you an attractive borrower and will open doors to more financial and employment opportunities in life.

If we accept the premise that obtaining and developing positive credit is good then why do so many bankruptcy filers stay away from credit after their bankruptcy case has been completed. There have been a number of studies on the reason why and here are the top four most common reasons:

a) They were hurt by using credit in the past.

b) They want to simplify their finances.

c) They don't understand the benefits of having good credit.

d) They lack understanding of the role of credit in society.

Most of us have been told that a "good credit score" is important. This is easy for us to understand, if something is good we are taught that is a good thing. It's common sense that you need to have a good credit to obtain a loan for a large purchase, however, today credit reports and credit scores are used for much more than just getting into a car loan or mortgage on a home.

Some of the lesser known reasons to have good credit:

a) **Paying for college**. Perhaps you're pursuing higher education right now. Maybe you have children and someday hope to send to college. Considering that the cost of college is rising faster than inflation, it's unlikely you will be able to pay for the tuition upfront you will need help financing the education.

b) **Renting**. A good credit rating can help you with finding a place to rent. Even if you've made the decision to entirely avoid credit and rent until you can write a check for a home, your credit still affects your housing because many landlords – particularly those in charge of higher-end housing – will check the credit ratings of potential renters and will reject (or charge a much higher deposit) from people who have no credit or poor credit.

c) **A good credit rating will help your insurance rates.** Insurance companies use your credit rating as a factor in determining what sort of rate to offer you on homeowners insurance, auto insurance, and life insurance. The higher your credit rating – meaning the more reliable you are at obtaining credit and then paying your bills faithfully – the better you appear as a risk to them. Lenders know that people with high credit scores are statistically more likely to be safe drivers, safe homeowners, and are more likely to live longer.

d) **Finding a job**. A good credit rating helps you with employment options. Today many employers run credit checks on potential employees and, again, are much more likely to hire people with strong credit because it's a clear indication that they are reliable.

e) **Credit often offers great buyer protection.** If you use credit to make a purchase – particularly credit cards – the card companies offer a lot of protection against fraud, identity theft, manufacture defects and other serious problems. If you pay cash, you miss out on those protections.

Bottom line is it pays to have a strong and positive credit score. Don't get me wrong, I'm not saying that it's good to be in debt creditors but that you need to get back in the credit game after filing bankruptcy if you want to thrive instead of merely survive financially down the road.

CREDIT REPORTING: HOW IT ALL STARTED

The Butcher, The Baker, The Candlestick Maker

Let's say in 1890 you were the local butcher and some new dandy rolls into town that wants to buy some of your specialty meats or maybe a whole side of beef and that sounds like a good thing. But there is a catch he wants to buy the products on credit and you know nothing about this stranger - what were you to do? He says he will pay you back but you have your concerns since the last guy that did this to you still owes you for his meat order that has never been paid. You think to yourself if he had done some past business with the local baker you could walk down the street and ask him about the new guy to see if he paid his bills on time and was worth the risk. If the Baker didn't know maybe you could go around the corner to the candlestick maker and get some information on the new guy from her. As cities grew and people became more and more mobile it became difficult to verify someone's reputation for repaying their debts...thus credit reporting was born more than 120 years ago, when a group of small retail merchants banded together to trade financial information about their customers.

The merchant associations then turned into small credit bureaus, which later consolidated into larger ones with the advent of computerization. By the 1960s, controversy surfaced over the Credit Associations as credit reports were being used to deny services and opportunities, and individuals had no right to see what was in their files. In addition, Credit Associations back then reported only negative financial information as well as "lifestyle" information culled from newspapers and other sources -- information such as sexual orientation, drinking habits, and cleanliness. The controversy led to a congressional inquiry, and in 1971, Congress passed the Fair Credit Reporting Act (FCRA), which established a framework for fair information practices to protect privacy and promote accuracy in credit reporting. Consumers gained the right to view, dispute and correct their records, and Credit Associations began to supplement the often-bleak reports with information on consumers' positive financial history.

However, it wasn't until 2001 that consumers gained direct access to their credit scores. Earlier that year, Consumer Reports had documented the problem of credit scores being off limits to consumers in an article entitled "New Assault on Your Credit Rating." The article, combined with growing pressures from lending institutions wanting to disclose scores to consumers, finally opened credit score information to individuals. An updated version of the FCRA, signed into law by President George W. Bush in December 2003, requires CRAs to provide consumers a copy of their credit score at a "fair and reasonable" fee.

Today's economy relies on the constant exchange of funds within the financial system and the increased buying power that credit provides. With credit, consumers can manage their cash flow, make purchases they may not otherwise be able to make, and in so doing, contribute to the economy's overall strength. However, the modern credit system would not be possible without the steady flow of borrower information, once obtained by word of mouth between the local butcher, baker and even the candlestick maker.

Simply stated, today a lender must be able to evaluate the likelihood that a borrower will repay the borrowed amount as agreed. Businesses that grant credit rely on tools like credit reports, credit scores, and other information solutions to assess the creditworthiness of a potential borrower.

TYPES OF CREDITORS

To understand credit and credit reporting you need to understand the different types of creditors. Each one of these creditors reports your history of repayment differently so it is also important to understand the different types of debt we are talking about. So let's focus on Secured versus Unsecured Creditors.

SECURED CREDITORS

What happens when a creditor lends money and the debt is not repaid? It's obvious: the creditor loses money. Instead of making a profit like they planned, they've taken a risk, lost and are placed in a difficult situation. The more creditors get burned, the less businesses and individuals are willing to take financial risks thus providing fewer opportunities for the rest of us to secure a payment on a home or obtain a better financial position in our lives. To prevent this scenario, secured creditors are asked to provide an added measure of security for the funds. Prior to signing an agreement with the borrower, secured creditors are granted a lien against an asset or piece of property that belongs to the debtor as terms of insurance. If the borrower fails to meet his obligations this asset is then turned over to the creditor which they can take and sell at the best price to make up for all or at least part of the loss they might have otherwise incurred.

A great example of this might be with a mortgage company. As a secured creditor the mortgage company agrees to give you a loan for a house, but if you fail to meet your payments they can foreclose on the property and reap the rewards of that process. Their loss is then at least partially made up by the income from that sale. Liens give creditors an added measure of security by enabling them to seize items of value to repay loans that go bad.

UNSECURED CREDITORS

On the other hand, unsecured creditors are not reimbursed with an individual's assets if the loan is not repaid. Money or services are given with the only assurance of the consumers promise to meet the required payment deadlines. Typical unsecured creditors in your day to day life might be the education system, hospital or your local dentist office. These groups cannot seize assets in the absence of payment. Same goes for your credit card company. They cannot repossess your car or foreclose on your house if you are unable to pay. Don't get me wrong, there are consequences for failing to repay a loan; however with the circumstances of unsecured creditors, they themselves are less likely to receive any form of immediate compensation.

CHAPTER TWO

WHAT HAPPENS ON YOUR CREDIT REPORT WHEN A BANKRUPTCY IS FILED?

Bankruptcy filings are a public record. The fact you filed for bankruptcy can legally be listed on your credit reports. As long as it is listed on your report your bankruptcy can impact your credit. The effect of having a bankruptcy on your report can be negative but in many situations you can actually turn it into a positive. It all depends where your credit score was at the time your bankruptcy case was filed.

If your credit history was considered healthy before the bankruptcy, it may be hit your report harder than someone with poor credit. Ultimately, how bankruptcy affects credit can vary, partially because of the various factors that make up your credit history and credit score that we will discuss more in depth later in this book.

According to the Fair Credit Reporting Act, a Chapter 7 bankruptcy may stay on your reports for 10 years from the date you file. A discharged Chapter 13 bankruptcy typically stays on your reports for seven years from the date you file, but it could remain for up to 10 years if you don't meet certain conditions. Both types have the same impact on your credit scores. However, it's possible that a future lender could view a Chapter 13 bankruptcy more favorably than a Chapter 7 bankruptcy.

Accounts included in a bankruptcy filing won't be reported as "unpaid" or "past due" anymore, and your credit history and score may feel relief without those financial issues being listed.

WHO LOOKS AT CREDIT REPORTS?

It's not only interesting but critical in your post-bankruptcy situation to know and understand the types of people and business that look at credit reports. Many parties look at your report on a fairly regular basis. Once you know who is looking at your credit report you can use this information to formulate a game plan to make sure your report portrays you and your situation in the best possible light. Most credit experts believe that 50 to 75% of all credit reports contain errors and other misinformation. In my experience I find it to be closer to the 75% range. Your reports could contain erroneous items that may impaction and prevent you from getting loans and/or interest rates that you should be entitled to. For example, your report could include negative items that belong to someone else and may neglect to include your own positive credit history. Hopefully you can see why it's important to know what is on your credit history.

From the website, *THE BALANCE*, the following list are some of the businesses and other entities that you can expect will be look at and monitoring you credit report.

a) **Current Lenders.** If you already have a credit card or loan, your creditor might check your credit report to decide whether to keep your account terms the same or to change them. If there is negative information on your credit report, your creditor might raise your interest rate, lower your credit limit or close your account completely. This comes as a surprise to many people since they think there is a right to a credit card or loan and it cannot just be taken away if you are making your payments on time. Businesses who you already do credit with don't need your express permission to check your credit report. The terms of your credit card or loan agreement likely include language letting you know the creditor will check your credit history periodically.

b) **Potential Creditors and Lenders.** When you apply for a new credit card or loan, the bank or lender will check your report first to decide whether to approve your application, to decide what credit limit or loan amount to give you, and to assign your loan an interest rate.

c) **Potential Landlords.** Many landlords check your credit report as part of the rental application process to determine whether or not they should rent to you. If you have recent delinquencies, foreclosures, or evictions on your credit report, your rental application could be denied.

d) **Your Insurance Company.** Insurance companies – even auto insurance companies - check your credit report to decide whether they should insure you and at what rate they should give you insurance. If you have negative information on your credit report, like late payments and collection accounts, you could have a higher insurance rate than consumers without negative information.

e) **A Prospective or Current Employer.** Potential employers use your credit report to make hiring decisions. Your current employer might also review your credit report before giving you a raise or promotion. Bankruptcy, account delinquencies, and high debt levels could keep you from getting a job or from getting a raise or promotion. Note that prospective employers check your credit report, not your credit score. They must also have your written permission before checking your credit report. Also note that you cannot be denied employment based on the fact you filed for bankruptcy – if you are told that is the reason you have been denied employment contact your bankruptcy attorney immediately.

f) **Debt Collectors**. Debt collectors view your credit report to get information that will help them collect the debt from you. This includes your current address and employer information. They may also view other accounts on your credit report to estimate whether you can pay the collection amount they will try to collect from you.

g) **Utility Services.** Before you can establish utilities, many companies will check your credit report. They may charge you a security deposit if there's information on your credit report that makes you look like a risky customer.

h) **Government agencies.** In certain circumstances, government agencies can check your credit report. For example to determine whether you qualify for public assistance, to calculate child support payments, or to process your application for a government license.

When these different entities look at your credit score they believe they are looking at a general snapshot of how reliable you are. Then they think they understand to what extent you are a financial risk and guess what kind of baggage you might bring to the table. Since this information can be very important to them and they are willing to pay a fair sum of money for your information. Hopefully you can now understand that you need to make sure your credit report presents you in the best possible light especially going forward after your bankruptcy.

WHAT DOES MY CREDIT REPORT ACTUALLY SAY ABOUT ME?

Let's first look at what kind of information is available on your credit report. Although each credit reporting agency formats and reports this information differently, all credit reports contain basically the same categories of information. There are four general categories listed in your credit report, each formatted and reported in a different way depending on the credit report agency.

IDENTIFYING INFORMATION

This will include your name, address, Social Security number, date of birth and employment information used to identify you. These factors are not used in credit scoring. Update to this information comes from the information you supply to lenders.

TRADE LINES

These are your credit accounts. Lenders report on each account you have established with them. They report the type of account (bankcard, auto loan, mortgage, etc.), the date you opened the account, your credit limit or loan amount, the account balance and your payment history.

CREDIT INQUIRIES

When you apply for a loan, you authorize your lender to ask for a copy of your credit report. This is how inquiries appear on your credit report. The inquiries section contains a list of everyone who accessed your credit report within the last two years. The report you see lists both "voluntary" inquiries, spurred by your own requests for credit, and "involuntary" inquiries, such as when lenders order your report so as to make you a pre-approved credit offer in the mail.

PUBLIC RECORD AND COLLECTIONS

Credit reporting agencies also collect public record information from state and county courts, and information on overdue debt from collection agencies. Public record information includes bankruptcies and civil lawsuits.

Your credit report does not just show how you pay your bills, it also shows whether you've been sued, arrested, filed for bankruptcy or have tax liens. I suggest once you get your credit report (I will tell you how to do that later in the book for free), you scan it for any discrepancy regarding delinquencies, loan balances and credit limits, unknown accounts or credit checks. If you find any mistakes immediately follow the steps listed later in the book to report the disputed facts and to request any needed corrections with the appropriate credit agency.

You should also write to the party that reported the inaccurate information to let them know you are disputing the information reported to the credit reporting agency. If you notice some unfamiliar accounts or requests for credit checks not initiated by you, you might have fallen victim to identity theft so immediately contact the credit reporting agencies and the police if it looks like your identity has been stolen.

Your credit report and your corresponding credit scores are meant to tell a creditor whether or not you're going to make a payment, not whether you can make a payment. This is an important distinction. But remember not every transaction in your life is reported on the credit report.

For example the following information sources will not appear on your credit report:

1. Unemployment benefits
2. Alimony
3. Child support
4. Public assistance benefits
5. Employment status
6. Spouse's credit history
7. Criminal past
8. Private medical information
9. Nontraditional loans
10. Pawned valuables
11. Payday loan
12. Car-title loans
13. Prepaid Debit Cards

Again, these types of transactions will not show up on your credit report. However if you default and the lender enlists a collection agency to come after you for the balance of one of these items then that action likely will go on to your report. Utility providers are also often missing from credit reports. While some power, gas and phone companies routinely report to credit bureaus and as a result, show up on your credit report. That can change if you dodge a bill that goes into collections. You can probably expect that notation to end up on your report.

FAQ:

WHY IS THERE NOTHING ABOUT MY NET WORTH ON A CREDIT REPORT?

A credit report is basically a list of all your current and recent past debts and obligations. Assets you own outright aren't included in the report. That means it doesn't include your net worth. There's nothing on a credit report that talks about how much money you have in the bank, the money you have in a brokerage account, your stock options or any other assets. If you own a piece of property free and clear, there's nothing on your credit report. The value of your home or home equity is also not on your report. The only related item that you could see is your mortgage, plus any loans or liens you have on the property.

THE DIFFERENCE BETWEEN A CREDIT REPORT AND A CREDIT SCORE

CREDIT REPORT

A credit report displays a window of your financial history with debts and other bill payments thus depicting your reliability as a consumer. Many people like to think of it as a "report card". This report can contain facts ranging from your personal information to specific details about your accounts. To name a few it includes: the types of accounts in your possession, age of your accounts, payment history, whether or not you have filed bankruptcy, collection actions outstanding debt, whether or not judgements have been entered against you, and any public record or collection items.

This report helps lenders understand what factors feed into the end credit score that everyone is concerned about. Because certain aspects of your financial habits are more important to lenders than others, having an opportunity to view your credit report enables them to feel more certain about the risks they may or may not take in a potential client.

CREDIT SCORE

A credit score is the analytical/numerical sum of your recent financial history. This number becomes a quick reference point for yourself, lenders, and landlords to gauge your creditworthiness. Unlike a Credit Report, your Credit Score does not display the list of actions that led to your current point status. For example, upon looking at your Credit Score, a lender is unable to tell what portion of it is contributed to the current amount of debt you owe, or how many lines of credit you hold. While details from your credit report are not displayed, many believe that the total number of points you do have can become a useful aide in predicting your financial behavior.

The website *BANKRATE,* provided the following chart that further illustrates the differences between the two:

	CREDIT REPORT	CREDIT SCORE
WHAT IS IT?	A credit report is a record of a consumer's credit history and serves as credit references.	A credit score is an algorithm that measures your credit risk based on the information in your credit report at one point in time.
WHO MAKES IT?	The three national credit reporting bureaus: Experian, Equifax and TransUnion.	FICO, Vantage Score and banks can create their own proprietary credit scores.
HOW MANY EXIST?	Three. Each bureau maintains one credit report on each person. The information in each report can differ because creditors don't have to report account information to all three.	There are 53 different FICO scores in existence. Once FICO 9 has been fully implemented over the next year or so, FICO will have a total of 65 scores. VantageScore maintains three generations of its credit score. There is an unknown number of bank proprietary scores in existence
CAN IT EXIST ALONE?	Yes, a credit report is a stand-alone document.	No, a credit score is calculated based on information in a credit report.
HOW DOES EACH JUDGE CREDITWORTHINESS?	Credit reports provide a detailed history of a person's current and past credit accounts and debt, third-party collections, certain public records and requests by lenders for the credit reports. The reports include dates accounts were opened, loan amounts, current balances and payment history, including late payments or defaults.	The most widely used credit score, FICO, considers five factors found in a credit report, each weighted differently, to arrive at the score. They are: payment history (35 percent); amounts owed (30 percent); length of credit history (15 percent); new credit (10 percent); and mix of credit (10 percent). Other credit scores use similar information, but may weight it differently and/or include other data.
HOW CAN I SEE IT?	Consumers are entitled to a free copy of their credit reports once every 12 months from each credit bureau under federal law. Free reports are available at AnnualCreditReport.com.	Mortgage lenders are required to show consumers the three credit scores that are pulled for the loan application. Other types of lenders also must disclose a credit score that was used to deny a consumer credit or to justify offering less-than-the-best terms. FICO and the credit bureaus offer educational credit scores, sometimes for free.

https://www.bankrate.com/finance/credit/credit-score-vs-credit-report-whats-what.aspx

CHAPTER THREE

KEY FACTORS TO A POSITIVE CREDIT REPORT

When you look at your credit report you will need to determine if you are on the right track moving towards a stable financial history or going backwards toward your pre-bankruptcy status?

Many of my former clients, who have successfully navigated the post-bankruptcy credit reporting process to get to a 700+ credit score, point to the following areas of concern they ran into rebuilding their credit history. I suggest as you move forward you keep an eye on the following area as you look to establish positive credit:

POSSIBLE CREDIT REPORT PROBLEM AREAS POST-BANKRUPTCY

No more than 11 accounts, open or closed	No more than one change of address and no name changes	Steady employment	Regular payments
No overdue payments	No defaults	No foreclosure	No late fees
Low (not zero) balances. And no large Balances	No balance rollovers	No accounts closed shortly after opening them	No open lines of credit

Bankruptcy Attorney Philip G Jones point out "If you have been guilty of any of these things. Do what you can to change now. Get the clocks ticking in your favor. Don't wait another day to begin improving your credit report."

Credit reports do not come with a credit score attached to it automatically. You actually have to pay for a "Credit Score". When you buy a credit score, most experts recommend that you get it from the Fair Isaac Corporation, or "FICO", as their scores are used in 90% of lending decisions. FICO takes information surrounding financial habits, analyze them, and then create a number that represents a score used to predict a consumer's behavior.

FICO is responsible for the analysis that determined how credit scores will be measured. This score helps lenders understand how likely an individual will be to turn a payment in on time, or whether or not they have the capacity to handle a larger line of credit.

The more understanding you have in relation to your FICO score the more intentional you can become in bettering your credit score. Myfico.com explains that 35% of your FICO score relates to your payment history, 30% relates to the amount of debt you owe, 15% relates to how long you've had your credit, 10% relates to new credit inquiries, 10% relates to your ability to manage different types of credit (mortgage, installment, revolving (credit card) and consumer finance). As you can see, staying on top of your debt and submitting payments on time dominates your FICO score outcome.

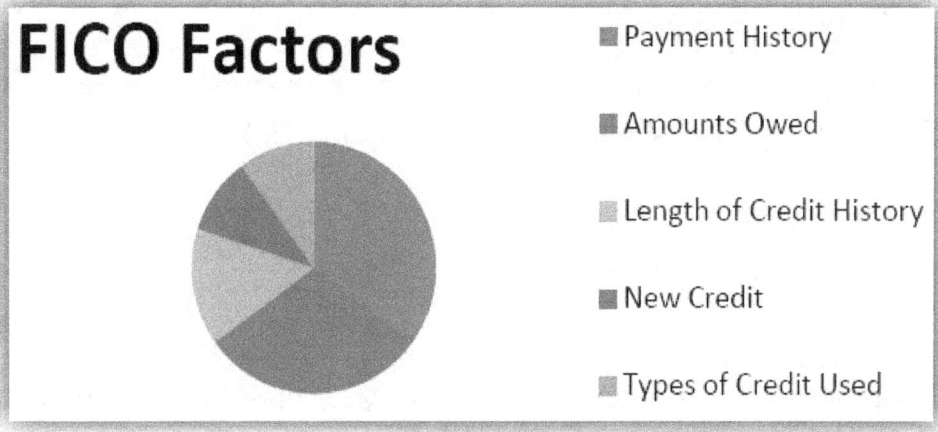

https://bpadvisors.com/how-do-i-look-what-does-my-credit-score-say-about-me/

3 MAJOR CREDIT REPORTING BUREAUS:

Credit Bureaus gather information about consumers throughout the country through reports and relevant public records that might list tax liens or bankruptcy information. Equifax, Experian, and Transunion are currently the largest credit bureaus in the United States. Their aim is to sell your information to creditors and others in a report. For example, a company to whom you've applied for credit with would have a valid need to look at your credit history. Your information can also be sold to companies that want to prescreen you for their products and services. These bureaus stay in business by competing against each other because of the differences in their data and the fact that they hold varying pieces to the puzzle of your financial history. These puzzle pieces create slightly different images which means that Equifax, Experian and Transunion actually have different credit scores under your name.

All this time we've been talking about your credit score -- you actually have *three* credit scores. You might find it typical of lenders to look at all three scores and base their decision off the median or middle score.

If you remember back to the story of *The Butcher, The Baker, The Candlestick Maker* in Chapter Two you will remember that credit bureaus were created to assist merchants and lenders in determining whether or not their potential clients were going to repay them their money. So while it's not required to report on your payments, it is within your creditors' best interest to report on your payment consistency or lack thereof. The varying amounts of information in the different bureaus come into play because creditors don't always want to take the time to report your payments to several different companies. Instead, depending on the creditor and what service they are rendering for you, they are likely to report to one credit bureau of their choice. Your financial information is spread around in a unique way between these giant bureaus owing to the fact that your financial life involves various creditors, lenders and landlords. At times this can be at a disadvantage to you because the good actions you take might slip between the cracks of the three companies--thus missing the opportunity to slightly raise your score.

HOW TO GET MY CREDIT REPORT

FOR FREE: visit www.annualreport.com

Under federal law you are entitled to a copy of your credit report annually from all three credit reporting agencies - Experian®, Equifax® and TransUnion® You can obtain all three of your reports at once, or space them out throughout the year.

Experian has created a personalized customer service that allows people to view their updated Experian credit report for free every 30 days online if you become a new member. See the link below.

https://usa.experian.com/#/registration?offer=at_fcras100&br=exp

For those of you who are already members:

Many people have already researched how you can get the same benefits, one of the main ways revolved around deleting your account and creating a new one, although, other options do exist. https://www.doctorofcredit.com/experian-now-offers-free-credit-monitoring-fico-score-report-free/#comment-271665

Equifax and **Transunion** by law permit an additional free credit report in the year for people who apply for and meet at least one of the following requirements:

- Persons receiving public welfare assistance;

- Persons who are unemployed and intend to apply for employment within 60 days,

- Persons who believe their credit report contains inaccurate information due to fraud.

You are also entitled to a free copy of your credit report if you meet these requirements:

- Persons who have been the subject of adverse action, such as denial of credit or insurance, within the past 60 days.

- Persons who have placed a fraud alert on their credit reports.

If any of these situations apply to you, you can request your additional free copy of your Equifax credit report:

- Online at Equifax.com/FCRA

- On our automated phone line: (800) 685-1111. Hours are 7:30 a.m. – 1:30 a.m. ET.

- By mail to: Equifax Disclosure Department, P.O. Box 740241, Atlanta, GA 30374.

And for the Transunion credit report:

- https://www.transunion.com/credit-reports-disclosures/free-credit-report

You will have to provide some personal information so the credit reporting agency can identify you.

Contact Information for Equifax, Experian, and TransUnion

To contact the three nationwide credit reporting agencies directly (to pay for additional reports):

Equifax

P.O. Box 740241
Atlanta, GA 30374-0241

800-685-1111
7:30 a.m. – 1:30 a.m. ET.

www.equifax.com

Experian

888-397-3742

www.experian.com

TransUnion

800-888-4213

www.transunion.com

TIPS FOR OBTAINING A REPORT:

It's a good idea to stagger your free credit reports throughout the year rather than requesting them from each of the 3 Credit Bureaus at once. That way you can watch your data and catch any suspicious activity before it's more than a few months old.

SPECIALTY REPORTS

There are a number of specialty reports that may be of interest to you depending upon for situation. For example:

Checking Accounts

Certegy/Equifax	800-437-5120
Check Center/CrossCheck	800-843-0760
CheckRite	800-766-2748
Check Systems	800-428-9623
International Check Services	800-526-5380
SCAN	800-262-7771
TeleCheck	800-710-9898

Rental Information

Accufax	800-256-8898
American Tenant Screen	800-888-1287
ChoicePoint Tenant History Reports	877-448-5732
National Tenant Network	800-228-0989
Tenant Data Services	800-228-1837
Tenant Screening Services	800-388-2335
UD Registry	818-785-3905

Mortgage Financing

Innovis	800-540-2505

TIP:

Each of these companies is obligated to provide you with an annual free copy of your credit report with them.

HOW TO CHALLENGE AN ERROR ON MY CREDIT REPORT

EXPERIAN:

ONLINE: https://www.experian.com/disputes/main.html

PHONE: To submit disputes by phone please call the number displayed on your credit report to speak with an agent. To request a copy of your personal credit report to be delivered by U.S. mail, call 1 866 200 6020

MAIL: You can dispute without a credit report by writing to Experian, P.O. Box 4500, Allen, TX 75013.

You can reference our Dispute by Mail PDF. This form can be mailed them or scanned and then uploaded to Experian.com/upload.

EQUIFAX:

ONLINE: http://www.equifax.com/personal/disputes

PHONE:1- 866-349-5191

MAIL: Equifax / P.O. Box / 740256 Atlanta, GA 30374-0256

TRANSUNION:

ONLINE: https://dispute.transunion.com

PHONE: 1-800-916-8800

Listed below is the nine step process created by Attorney Phil Jones on how to dispute errors on your credit report:

1) Review Your Credit Report

   Once you have received copies of your credit reports you must carefully review them for accuracy. First, check all of your personal information. Ensure that your name is spelled correctly. If any variations of your name appear that you have not applied for credit under, you will want to object to them. Make sure your social security number is correct. Also check any reported addresses for accuracy. Then, check your credit information. Ensure that all your accounts are listed. If an account is not listed, would it help you to have it included? Look for any errors in reference to any of your accounts. Look for accounts that are not yours. Look for multiple accounts as a result of bank or store mergers. And look for unused overdraft accounts.

2) Step 2 - Prioritize the Errors

   The next step is to find no more than three errors that you think will be (1) the easiest to prove and (2) are hurting your credit the worst. The credit bureaus apparently take your disputes more seriously if you only dispute a few items at a time. The following is a recommended order in which you should object to erroneous items on your credit report:
   Personal Information
   Bankruptcy
   Foreclosure
   Repossession
   Loan Default

Court Judgment
Collections
30 Days Late
More than 30 Days Late
Credit Rejections
Credit Inquiries

It is often wise to dispute incorrect personal information first. Collection company errors should probably be disputed last. The reason to fix the personal information first is that the collection error may be resolved by merely correcting a bad address or other identifying number.

3) **Gather Information**

Once you have determine what you are going to dispute it will be necessary to gather information that can be presented to the bureaus as proof of the errors you are bringing to their attention. If you are disputing your name or birth date, you will need a copy of your driver's license. If you are disputing your social security number you will need a copy of the Social Security Card. It is also helpful to include your credit report confirmation number with any dispute.

4) **Keep a Log**

As you begin the process of improving your credit report it will be very important to keep accurate records of each step you take. Be sure to keep a log of every letter you send, every phone call you make, every letter you receive, and every call you receive. Be sure to note the names and titles of any individuals you speak with.

5) **Dispute Incorrect Information**

The next step is to prepare a dispute letter. Address your letter as follows:

Equifax Information Services LLC
PO Box 740256
Atlanta, GA 30374

Experian
PO Box 2104
Allen, TX 75013-2104

TransUnion Consumer Solutions
PO Box 2000
Chester, PA 19022-2000

6) Address Each Concern

Be sure to address each concern in a separate paragraph. As indicated above, limit yourself to the top three items on your list of errors. The credit bureau also needs to know if you are challenging something because it is not yours or because you were not late. Normal types of disputes include:

Accounts Not Yours	Didn't Pay Late	Account Closed	Fraudulent Account
Fraudulent Charge	Account in Bankruptcy	Paid in Full	Paid before Collections or Charge off

7) Indicate your Objection

Indicate whether you are objecting to the "existence of a listing" or the "information within a listing". When disputing a specific account the following is a recommended order:
Wrong Amount
Wrong Account Number
Wrong Original Creditor
Wrong Charge-off Date
Wrong Last Date of Activity
Wrong Balance
Wrong Credit Limit
Wrong Status
Wrong High Credit

It is usually not very helpful to challenge errors within something that is negative. For example, the address of a property that was foreclosed. The bureau will also need a reason for your dispute. Also be sure to indicate what you want the credit bureau to do. It is usually best to ask for "deletion" rather than "correction" of an item. Send your letter certified mail, return receipt requested. Be sure to keep your receipts.

8) **Wait for a Response**

The credit bureau has 30 days in which to investigate your dispute and respond to you. The FCRA requires the bureau to notify you within five days of completing their investigation. They must remove any item that cannot be verified or where they decide that you are correct.

If an item is removed from your credit report, they must provide you with a copy of the corrected report. If they determine that the item was correct, no change will be made.

If you do not receive a response within 30 days, it is important to send an immediate request for reinvestigation. If for some reason you get a letter from the bureau requesting more information you should not respond. The credit bureau may be trying to buy extra time. If you answer their letter they have an additional 15 days to complete their investigation. However, you should keep a copy of the letter since it may be helpful later.

If you get no response to your request for reinvestigation, you should file a complaint with the FTC. Go to the following web address to file your complaint.

Http://rn.ftc.gov/pls/dod/wsolcq$.startup?Z_ORG_CODE=PU01

Sometimes your credit report will be corrected and then the item will reappear later. As a result it is important to request a new credit report a few months after you take corrective action. If the error reappears you should send a letter to the credit bureau. The credit bureau is required to notify you within five days of replacing any negative information on your credit report. Failure to notify you is a violation of the law that can subject them to financial penalties.

WHAT HAPPENS AFTER YOU DISPUTE INFORMATION ON YOUR CREDIT REPORT?

According to the Consumer Financial Protection Bureau:

Credit reporting companies must investigate your dispute, forward all documents to the furnisher, and report the results back to you unless they determine your claim is frivolous. If the consumer reporting company or furnisher determines that your dispute is frivolous, it can choose not to investigate the dispute so long as it sends you a notice within five days saying that it has made such a determination.

If the furnisher corrects your information after your dispute, it must notify all of the credit reporting companies it sent the inaccurate information to, so they can update their reports with the correct information.

If the furnisher determines that the information is accurate and does not update or remove the information, you can request the credit reporting company to include a statement explaining the dispute in your credit file. This statement will be included in future reports and provided to whoever requests your credit report.

> **TIP:**
>
> If you suspect that the error on your report is a result of identity theft, visit Identity Theft.gov, the federal government's one-stop resource to help you report and recover from identity theft.

WHY DO SOME CREDITORS NOT SHOW UP ON MY CREDIT REPORT?

Just because a creditor does not appear on your current report doesn't mean that it won't be reported on the report in the future. Over time you'll also begin to notice that not all companies report to the credit reporting agencies--most major lenders and creditors do, but not all of them. I find that smaller merchants like small landlords, dentist and doctors usually do not report to the agencies unless they send your account to a debt collector for non or slow payment.

HOW LONG WILL IT TAKE TO RAISE MY CREDIT SCORE?

BANKRATE supplied this example: A missed mortgage payment can lower your credit score by 50 percent, but your score can recover within 1.5 years if you manage your credit well during that time period.

HOW LONG WILL BANKRUPTCY BE REPORTED ON A CREDIT REPORT?

According to the *Fair Isaac Corporation*, or FICO, the typical length of time different types of negative information remain on your credit report is as follows:

- Late payments: 7 years.

- Bankruptcies:

  - 7 years for completed Chapter 13 bankruptcies

  - 10 years for Chapter 7 bankruptcies

- Foreclosures: 7 years

Bankruptcy becomes a derogatory item on your credit report and can stay there for up to seven years. Having a 'derogatory' item on your report damages your creditworthiness.

According to *VantageScore Solutions*, the impact of a derogatory item on your credit score decreases with time.

CHAPTER FOUR

WHAT DO THE NUMBERS MEAN ON MY CREDIT SCORE?

SUPERPRIME: 781 – 850

A score between 781 and 850 is a GREAT place to be. It's easy to see that you are consistent and responsible with managing loans and payments. Consumers within this block of numbers are able to get competitive interest rates on mortgages, loans and credit lines. Scores of 800+ are especially good and can only be reached with a long history of no late payments, and steady low balances on credit cards. At this point you are clearly a low risk for defaulting on your credit agreements.

PRIME: 661-780

As far as U.S consumers go this range places you as average or slightly above it. The national average FICO score is 695. At this point you are unlikely to be kept from qualifying for credit, but some ideal rates will be just out of reach and may cost you higher interest rates on loans. If you place above 750 you are likely to qualify for the best rates on loans of any kind.

NEAR PRIME: 601 – 660

Some would consider 601-660 as a fair credit score. There are dings and dents on your credit score perhaps from things such as carrying a tall balance on your credit cards, or tardiness in paying bills but nothing that suggests major delinquencies. However with a score between 600 and 660 you are unlikely to get competitive rates towards your credit. Near prime suggests that you are going through some rough credit times or recovering from recent setbacks.

SUBPRIME: 300 – 600

An individual with a score between 300 and 600 is in a poor situation with significantly damaged credit history. This score range notifies lenders and landlords alike that you are not in a good place and too big of a risk. A chance of getting new credit is slim.

ADDITIONAL WAYS TO BOOST YOUR CREDIT

You now have a great opportunity to write a new credit history. Since you filed for bankruptcy you should have emerged from the process with no unsecured debts and very few secured debts. You may still owe student loans, child support and possibly past due tax debt but you have shed a whole lot of the major problems that effected your credit. In this chapter I want to explain in depth a few highly successful ways to restore rebuild and renew your credit. These will be referred to later on as we start to come up with your Game Plan to get your life bank after bankruptcy.

SECURED LINES OF CREDIT

One way to start improving your credit score is to open a secured credit card account right after you receive a discharge in your bankruptcy. You will need to go to a bank, fill out an application and make a deposit into a secured account. The bank, in turn, provides a credit card with a credit line that's 50% to 100% of the deposit. The Federal Trade Commission says that the bank will usually pay interest on your deposit.

Note: Read the fine print some secured cards come with an annual fee. Also sometimes the annual percentage rates for secured credit cards may range from 15% to 23%, rates that are higher than most unsecured cards. At this point you need to do your homework and find a bank with low fees and interest on their secured credit cards.

Be prepared to pay application and processing fees, and check to see whether you will get a refund if you're denied the card. Compare the total fees required before signing anything.

Also, confirm that the bank reports your credit card limit to the major credit card bureaus, offers periodic credit increases and doesn't report the card as secured. See https://www.bankrate.com/finance/debt/bankruptcy-timeline-rebuilding-credit-1.aspx

Here's how it works:

When you're approved for a savings secured line of credit, your bank gives you access to a pool of money that you can use to pay for minor expenses up to an established amount. In exchange, the bank holds funds in your savings account as collateral. When you pay back the money and close your line of credit, the hold on your savings account is lifted; until then, you can continue borrowing and repaying money.

If you wanted a $5,000 line of credit, we'd make sure you had at least $5,000 in your savings account, then we'd put a hold on those funds and issue you a line of credit you can obtain savings secured lines of credit with as little as $250 and as much as $10,000 in a savings account.

WHAT ARE THE BENEFITS?

A savings secured line of credit can be attractive for many reasons the advantages include:

⦿ **Flexibility:** You can use your line of credit for whatever you need — a monthly bill due before you receives your paycheck, an emergency car repair, or even a vacation.

⦿ **Interest accrual:** When you use your savings secured line of credit, your savings stay in your account, continuing to earn interest.

⦿ **Quick approval:** Banks typically make a decision on applications within a couple of hours; with a conventional loan or line of credit, a decision could take days or even weeks.

⦿ **Competitive interest rates:** When banks issue secured credit, the availability of your collateral, to the bank, means they are taking on less risk. As a result, they may offer more favorable interest rates than they would with unsecured credit.

⦿ **Generous credit criteria:** Savings secured lines of credit typically have less stringent underwriting criteria. As a result, individuals can often qualify even if they have no credit or weak credit, from bankruptcy or other circumstances.

WHAT ARE THE DISADVANTAGES?

⦿ **Small credit amounts:** Because of the relatively low balances, ($400 to $600) savings secured lines of credit typically cannot be used for big-ticket purchases.

⦿ **Limited access to savings:** Once you take out a savings secured line of credit, your savings are held by the bank until you pay back the line of credit.

Ultimately a savings secured line of credit can be a safety net for people who need cash flow or a stepping stone for those who want to work on improving their creditworthiness. Since you are responsible for paying back the borrowed amount as well as the interest accrued it is essential to manage what you borrow responsibly.

The intent of a savings secured line of credit isn't to help you go out and make a major purchase you can't afford. It's to give you easy access to funds when you need them, and help you build or rebuild your credit profile by borrowing and paying back relatively small amounts on a regular basis.

> **TIP:**
>
> Start immediately- The faster you start, the faster you will see positive results. This sounds obvious, but taking action is very difficult for many people.

DISPUTE CREDIT CARD BILLING ERRORS

Be sure to review all your billing statements each month. If you see any errors you should immediately contact the store where the charge was made. If they will not help, then you should contact the customer service department of your credit card regarding your concerns. Be sure to include all of the steps you took to resolve the matter with the store making the incorrect charge. You must complain within 60 days of the statement date to preserve your rights. The service department then has 30 days in which to respond under the Fair Credit Billing Act. Send your letter certified, return receipt requested. Be sure to keep copies of everything.

OPT OUT

The credit bureaus sell your information to companies that want to offer you credit. You can request that they no longer give out your information. Send a request to opt out letter to the following addresses:

Equifax Options PO Box 740123 Atlanta, GA 30374-0123	Experian Consumer Opt Out 701 Experian parkway Allen, TX 75013	TransUnion Marketing List Opt Out PO Box 97328 Jackson, MS 39288-7328

You should also call 1-888-567-8688 to prevent them from giving information to "pre-screened offers".

You can also stop unsolicited mailings from any member of the Direct Marketing Association by sending a letter to:

Mail Preference Service
Attn: Dept 26714550
Direct Marketing Association
PO Box 282
Carmel, NY 10512

There is a $1 fee to opt out. You can also go to their web site at:

www.the-dma.org/consumers/offmailinglist.html
www.dmaconsumers.org/cgi/offmailing

You can reduce unwanted email solicitation from members of the Direct Marketing Association by going to:

www.dmaconsumers.org/offemaillist.html and
www.e-mps.org

If you want to reduce phone solicitations by members of the Direct Marketing Association write to:

Telephone Preference Service
Direct Marketing Association
PO Box 9014
Farmingdale, NY 11735

Other organizations to write to in order to reduce your junk mailings can include:

First Data Info-Source Donnelley Marketing, Inc. Database Operations 235 "N" Ave. Nevada, IA 50201	Database America Compilation Dept. 100 paragon Dr. Montvale, NJ 07645	R. L. Polk & Co. List Compilation 26955 Northwestern Highway South Field, MI 48034	Metromail Corp. List Maintenance 901 West Bond Lincoln, NE 68521
Acxiom Corporation Opt-Outs/Consumer Advocacy PO Box 2000 Conway, AR 72033-2000	Abacus Direct PO Box 1478 Broomfield, CO 80038-1478	InfoUSA Product Quality PO Box 27347 Omaha, NE 68127	Donnelly Marketing, Inc. Database Operations 416 S. Bell Ames, IA 50010

Remember that your opt outs are usually only good for one to five years and you will then need to repeat the process. You should also never open emails from parties that you do not recognize. There are many people out there attempting to defraud you. They will even pretend to be from your bank or credit card company. Never give personal information like your account number, social security number, pin number, etc. over the internet. If you get a request for such information, call the creditor immediately to report the contact. The creditor's security department will want as much information about the contact as you can give them.

BONUS TIP:

For IOS and Android users: There is a new App circulating called 'PINCH'. This is a free service and currently the app is also free. Pinch is a consumer app that lets people use their rent payments as proof of their good credit without having to go through a landlord. Typically, Landlords don't take the time to report your rental payments to credit bureaus. But if your payments were to be used as proof of consistent payment and good credit, your credit score would likely receive a noticeable boost. More information can be found at www.pinchrent.com

THINGS THAT CANNOT BE DONE

Beware of several scams out there that claim they can "clean" your credit without you doing anything other than paying them a fee. As my colleague Phillip Jones, is fond of saying, there are no guarantees. No one can promise to fix your credit report. There are too many variables, including an employee who may refuse to read the letter sent to the credit bureau. Second, bankruptcies, judgments, liens, and bad loans generally cannot be removed from your credit report. You have no right to challenge correct information. The only way to fix these kinds of items is to let time pass or obtain the assistance of the creditor involved. Third, you cannot improve your credit by creating a new identity. Some companies will encourage you to apply for a new tax identification number, falsify part of your social security number, or use someone else's name. Each of these things is a violation of the law and will cause you more problems than bad credit will. Fourth, you cannot buy a clean credit report. Some companies will inundate the credit bureau with multiple disputes counting on the credit bureau not being able to respond in time. The offending item will be removed, you will be shown a clean credit report, and you think you are home free. However, within the next 30 to 120 days, the offending material shows back up on your credit report as the bureau completes their investigation or creditors update their information. Quick fixes do not work in the long run anyway. It is best to proceed carefully and cautiously in correcting errors on your credit report, and to take those personal steps that will improve your credit. In addition to rebuilding your credit many of these steps are great life skills that will help you well beyond the short rebuilding time after your bankruptcy.

CHAPTER FIVE

YOUR GAME PLAN TO REBUILD, RESTORE, AND RENEW YOUR CREDIT AFTER BANKRUPTCY

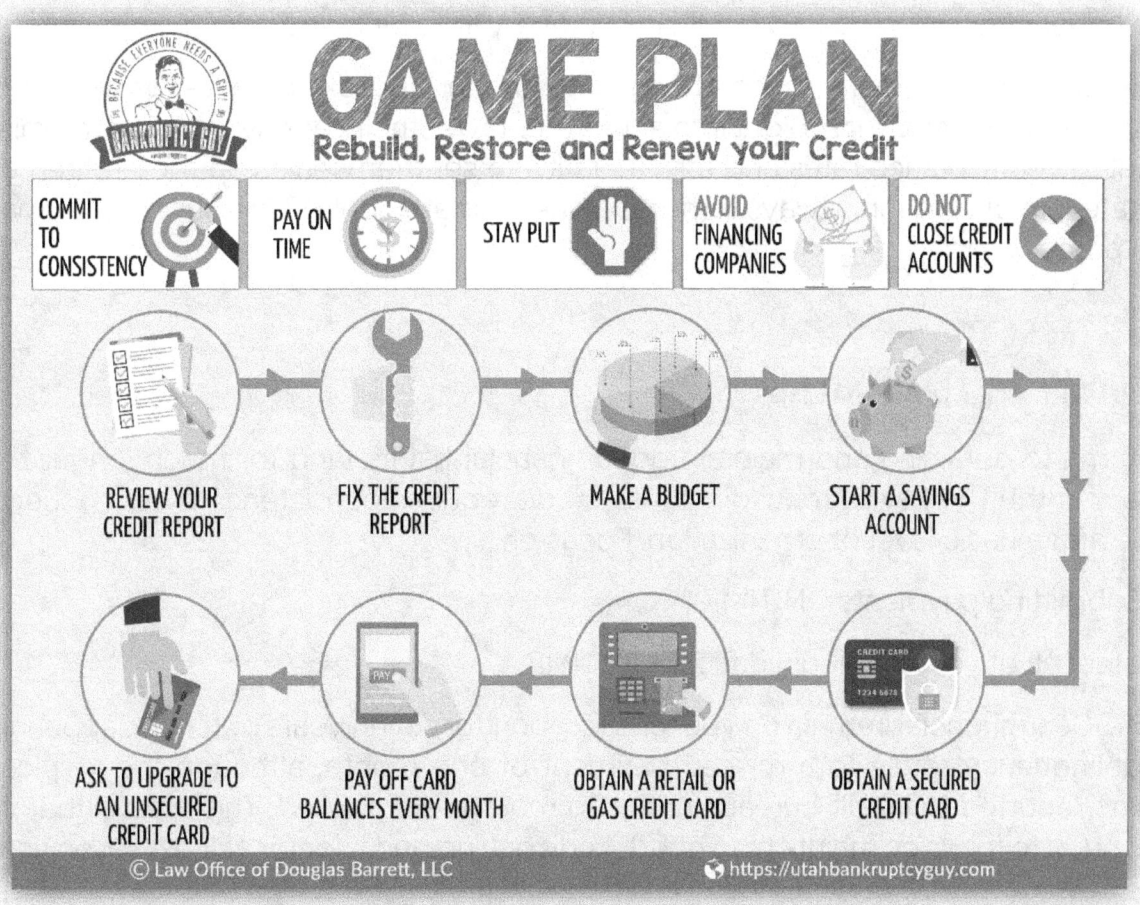

With everything you've learned up to this point—ranging from understanding credit bureaus, to disputing errors on your credit history—it's time to start on your new financial future. Bankruptcy may have given you a clean slate but now it's your job to present your best case to potential creditors showing that you are worthy of their trust. Show them why they should lend you money; give them evidence that reassures them that they will be repaid. Now is the time to put on your game face and present yourself in the best possible light.

The following Game Plan has 13 steps to use at your discretion. In some cases a credit report will not need corrections thus enabling you to skip over the second step. Clearly some of the steps will not apply to everyone. Focus on the areas that you may have had problems with in the past such as budgeting and/or paying your debts on time. I know that budgeting is commonly disliked but it is a critical key to your future financial stability and so are the other steps in this plan. As you work towards that 720 credit score, don't make the mistake of overlooking the seemingly small things. Believe it or not, the "small things" may have just as big of an impact on your score as the larger concrete steps. To put it simply: every little bit helps.

As you commit to make these changes it is important to remember what you are working for. For some it's to get into a home, or lower their car payments, some might want lower insurance rates and for others it's to set themselves up for a retirement. Whatever your reason, always remember the ultimate goal – it is a sure way to make the process easier.

1. COMMIT TO CONSISTENCY.

Commit to obtaining and maintain good financial habits (and for much longer than one month). The key to rebuilding your credit requires consistency over a period of time and a basic level of organization. Focus on:

a) Submitting payments ON TIME

b) Meet all of your credit obligations ON TIME

Note: Delinquencies remain on your credit report for seven years before disappearing. A delinquency refers to a missed payment of one month, although they typically aren't reported to credit bureaus until two months are missed. This means that you will need to focus on maintaining good credit paying behavior for at least seven years.

c) Organization. Consistency with finances requires a basic level of organization. You need to know when your payments are due and then make sure the payments are paid on time. Otherwise slow or missed payments will be reported and hurt your credit history.

2. REVIEW YOUR CREDIT REPORT.

Review the credit report you received when your bankruptcy case was filed.   If for some reason you did not get a credit report when you filed bankruptcy get one ASAP since you need to have a baseline to start from as you move through this process. Know exactly where you stand with regards to credit, and how far you need to go to get to the credit score you want. In addition to your credit report, review your credit score. Typically anything over 700 is considered good, with 750 — 850 considered excellent. Conversely, anything under 640 is considered poor with 400 or lower being very poor. Knowing this helps inform you how drastically your finances need to be restructured.

3. FIX YOUR CREDIT REPORT.

You will need to take the steps to challenge any bad information on your credit report. If you are lucky there is no bad or misinformation present on your credit history but it is not uncommon for incorrect information to appear on your credit report (or for there to be inconsistencies between reports by different bureaus). For example, debts that are paid in full could be listed as unpaid, or incorrect payment history could be present. Bankruptcy can negatively affect your credit score for up to 10 years so you need to fix all other items possible on the credit report now to get to a higher score.

4. STAY PUT.

If at all possible try to keep your same address for as long as possible. A portion of your credit score is based on your stability. The statisticians at FICO know that a borrower who has lived in their home for 20 years is less likely to default than a renter who moves every six months to a year. Although it's a small portion of what goes into your score, every little thing counts at this point of the process.

5. MAKE A BUDGET.

Proper budgeting skills are the first step in building strong financial habits that will not only help you rebuild credit, but also help you maintain good credit going forward. This will also help prevent financial hardship in the future. Budgeting allows you to know what money comes in, and make a strict plan for what goes out. The golden rule of budgeting is to never spend more than you make. If you are, this means spending needs to be reduced, or income needs to be increased.

6. START A SAVINGS ACCOUNT.

Build savings into your budget. Once you know how much you make and how much you spend, it is important to reduce non-essential expenses as much as possible. This will leave more room for on-time bill payments (an essential part of rebuilding credit), free up cash for repaying loans in a timely manner, and allow for savings every month. The key is to be aware of what you **want** versus what you **need**, and to reduce needs as much as possible. Make sure to look closely at your needs as well, and confirm they are not wants. Every month, it is important to put a little bit away in savings. Although 5 to 10% is recommended, saving anything is positive. Having emergency savings allows you to forgo using credit if there a sudden bill that emerges.

As part of your savings have an emergency fund. You need this now more than ever. Having a small emergency fund, of as little as $300, can prevent nearly 80% of the negative things that end up going onto most credit reports. Always remember that after you dip into your emergency fund you need to replace it as soon as possible otherwise the negative credit history cycle that you are trying to change may once again plague your credit reports.

7. PAY ON TIME.

Once you have created your personal budget you will have a much clearer image of your expenses. It is important to prioritize your expenses so that all bills are paid exactly when they are due. Payment history makes up 35% of your credit score, and on-time repayments can quickly and easily rebuild a damaged credit score.

8. OBTAIN A SECURED CREDIT CARD.

Unlike a debit card that directly draws money from your bank account, a credit card allows you to borrow money and pay it over time. This is the easiest way to start rebuilding credit. A secured credit card involves giving the bank money (say $500), and then the bank gives you credit in that amount. Secured credit cards are typically offered through banks, although some credit card companies like Discover also offer secured credit cards. Make sure to keep in mind the following:

a. Start with around $500. As your credit improves, ask the bank or credit union if you can slowly start raising the limit.

b. Be wary of anyone that asks you for outrageous start-up fees (some places try to charge up to $200) or for you to call a 1-900 number that will charge you money. Some lenders specifically seek out recently filed bankruptcies since they cannot seek court protection again for eight years. Don't open more than one or two of these types of accounts.

c. Be sure to ask if your transactions will be reported to all three major credit bureaus. You want them to see that you're paying off your debts so your score can begin to improve.

d. Know that some banks might force you to wait for a year after you've filed bankruptcy to get a secured card. If that is the case, look for another bank or credit union that is more willing to work with you in your situation.

e. Get a secured card at a bank or credit union you want to continue to use for a while. You'll eventually want to ask the bank if you can switch to an unsecured card with the same bank, so choose wisely.

9. OBTAIN A RETAIL OR GAS CREDIT CARD.

Once you are on track with the secured credit card, you should try applying for a retail or gas credit card. This is important to improving your credit because one aspect of your credit score is "types of credit in use." By using different types of credit, you improve your credit score. Keep these points in mind when you're looking into it:

a. Make sure your transactions will be reported to all three credit bureaus. Remember, the point of all this is for them to see you being responsible with your money.

b. Avoid huge start-up fees.

c. Try to get a card at a store where you won't be tempted to go on a shopping spree. Gas cards are a good idea because gas is a necessary expense that you won't be tempted to splurge on. Try to avoid department stores that might lure you into trouble with expensive items that are out of your price range.

d. Along with retail and gas cards (which are typically accessible to people with poor credit), eventually adding other types of credit can go a long way to improve your credit rating. These other types of credit include installment loans (like a line of credit, or car loan) or mortgages. If you do not already have loans in these categories, it is very wise to wait at least two years after bankruptcy to consider a car loan, mortgage, or line of credit.

10. PAY OFF CARD BALANCES EVERY MONTH.

You may have been told that carrying a credit card balance is great for your credit score, but that's not necessarily true. Especially if you have bad credit, the credit bureaus want to see that you're capable of paying off the balance as often as necessary. Keep in mind that 35% of your credit score is payment history, so paying bills on-time and in-full will quickly build your credit.

11. DO NOT CLOSE CREDIT ACCOUNTS.

As mentioned earlier, 35% of your credit score is dependent on payment history and another 30% is based on the different amounts you owe. This is calculated by looking at how much you owe relative to how much credit you have available. When you close accounts, your total credit limit decreases this in turn lowers your credit score. Additionally the more varied the types of credit accounts you have the more attractive you will look to the credit reporting companies.

12. AVOID FINANCING COMPANIES.

Finance companies exist to make a profit. Most of them make huge profits. The vast majority of them charge well above the market rates on their loans. It is especially important to avoid check loan and/or pay day lenders.

Instead of being swayed by debt consolidation offers, focus on maintaining your budget, putting money into savings, and slowly building up the limit on your secured card or retail card.

13. ASK TO UPGRADE TO AN UNSECURED CREDIT CARD.

Once you have successfully managed a secured card for more than 12 months, ask your bank if you can switch over to an unsecured card. Most banks will agree to letting you have a low-limit unsecured card after 12 to 24 months. Keep the same mentality you had with the secured card. Avoid spending money you don't have on the unsecured card so that you can keep yourself from sliding into bankruptcy again.

> **TIP:**
> Remember the point of this Game Plan is to let the credit bureaus know you are capable of repaying your debts--don't let them see anything different!

42

ABOUT THE AUTHOR

Douglas Barrett, Attorney and Counselor at Law

Mr. Barrett received his undergraduate degree from Brigham Young University (BA '93), holds a certificate in International Law from the University of the Pacific, McGeorge School of Law ('99) and is a graduate of Whitter Law School (JD '00).

During law school Mr. Barrett was an extern Law Clerk to the Hon. James N. Barr, United States Bankruptcy Court for the Central District of California. After graduating from Whitter Law School, Mr. Barrett served as Law Clerk to the Hon. Lee M. Jackwig, United States Bankruptcy Court for the Southern District of Iowa.

Upon completing this clerkship, Mr. Barrett returned to his home town to open a law office catering to the individual needs of his clients. Having been raised most of his life in Utah, Mr. Barrett understands the unique social, business, and legal community of the State of Utah.

Mr. Barrett is a member of the National Association of Consumer Bankruptcy Attorney's (NACBA), the Utah Bar Association (UBA), and the Central Utah Bar Association (CUBA). Mr. Barrett has been recognized as one of the Legal Elite - Bankruptcy Attorneys in the State of Utah, by his peers, in Utah Business Magazine for ten consecutive years. In 2017 the U.S. Patent Office issued him the Trademark as "The Bankruptcy Guy." He was recently recognized by the online referral service AVVO as a Top-Rated Attorney.

Mr. Barrett is also the author of the books:

THE INSIDERS GUIDE: Getting a Fresh Financial Start in Utah

LIFE AFTER BANKRUPTCY: The Game Plan to Rebuild, Restore and Renew your Credit after Bankruptcy